Mae Jemison
ASTRONAUT

Written by Garnet Nelson Jackson
Illustrated by Fred Willingham

MODERN CURRICULUM PRESS

Program Reviewers

Leila Eames, Coordinator of Instruction,
    Chapter 1
    New Orleans Public Schools
    New Orleans, Louisiana

Stephanie Mahan, Teacher
    Bethune Elementary School
    San Diego, California

Thomasina M. Portis, Director
    Multicultural/Values Education
    District of Columbia
    Public Schools
    Washington, D.C.

Modern Curriculum Press
An imprint of Pearson Learning
299 Jefferson Road, P.O. Box 480
Parsippany, NJ 07054 - 0480

http://www.pearsonlearning.com

ISBN 0-8136-5239-1 (Reinforced Binding)   0-8136-5245-6 (Soft Cover)

Library of Congress Catalog Card Number: 93-79426

Dear Readers,

Do you ever dream of being something special when you grow up? Mae Jemison did. Why, she knew she wanted to be an astronaut when she was only five years old.

Her mother and father helped. Her teachers helped.

But mostly, Mae helped herself. Read to find out how hard work can make your dreams come true.

Your friend,

Garnet Jackson

Both asleep and awake, Mae Jemison had dreams of traveling in outer space among the stars and planets.

When she was five years old, Mae told her teacher in Chicago, Illinois, that she would be a scientist when she grew up.

Mae knew that an astronaut had to understand science. So she wanted to study science and never stopped dreaming about traveling in outer space.

3

4

In 1965, when Mae was eight years old, the United States was sending astronauts into space. Mae watched the first Gemini flights on television. Her heart pounded with excitement.

Mae pictured herself on the flights. "One day," she thought. "One day."

Mae's parents, Dorothy and Charles
Jemison, knew of their daughter's dream.
To help Mae learn more about science,
they took her, with her older brother and
sister, to the library.

While reading books, Mae spent hours and hours traveling through space. When she was not reading, she enjoyed playing sports and dancing with her friends.

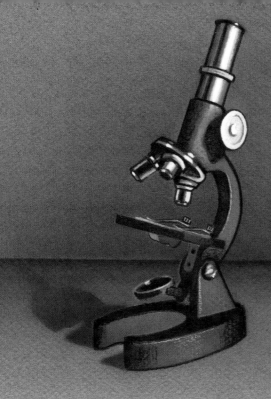

Her parents told Mae that she had to work extra hard in school to make her dreams come true. Mae followed their advice.

She graduated from high school at age sixteen. She had done so well that Stanford University asked her to attend college there for free.

In college, Mae wanted to learn
everything about her world. To become
a scientist, she studied chemistry and
biology. To learn about her ancestors,
she studied about Africa.

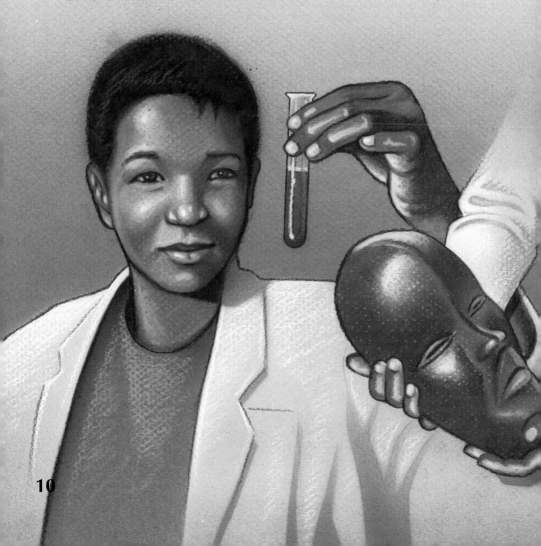

When Mae graduated from Stanford University, she decided to help sick people. So she went to Cornell University to study to be a doctor.

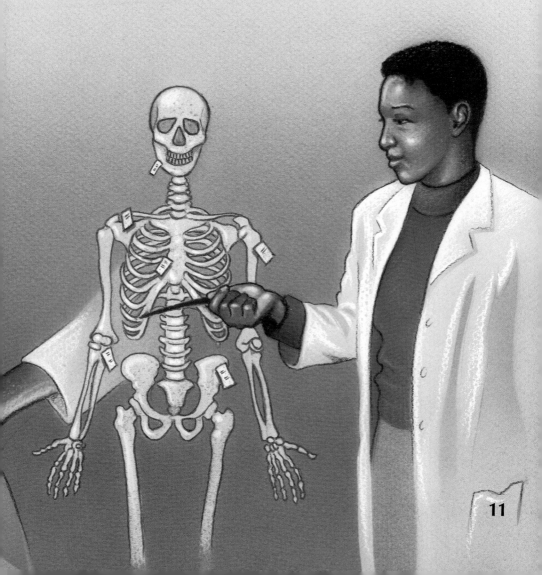

Soon after she became Dr. Jemison, Mae went to West Africa. There she helped Peace Corps workers in Sierra Leone and Liberia.

But Mae's dream to become an astronaut was still alive. In 1985 she wrote to NASA, the group that trains astronauts. She asked to be a part of the space program.

NORTH
AMERICA

UNITED
STATES

ATLANTIC
OCEAN

AFRICA

SIERRA
LEONE
LIBERIA

N
W · E
S

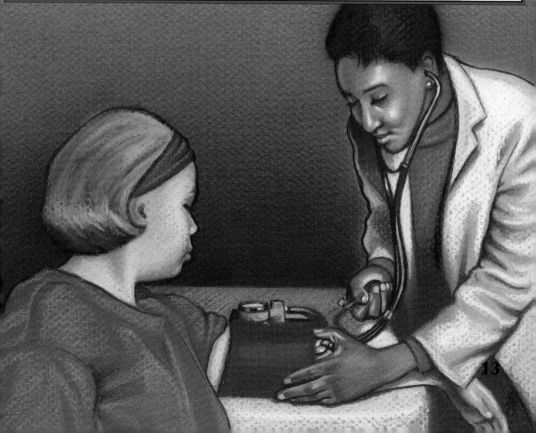

13

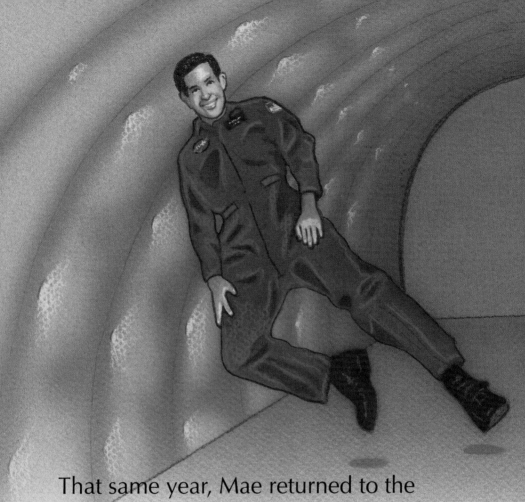

That same year, Mae returned to the
United States to work as a doctor in
Los Angeles.

Two years later, she got the news she
had been waiting for! NASA had chosen
Mae to train to be an astronaut.

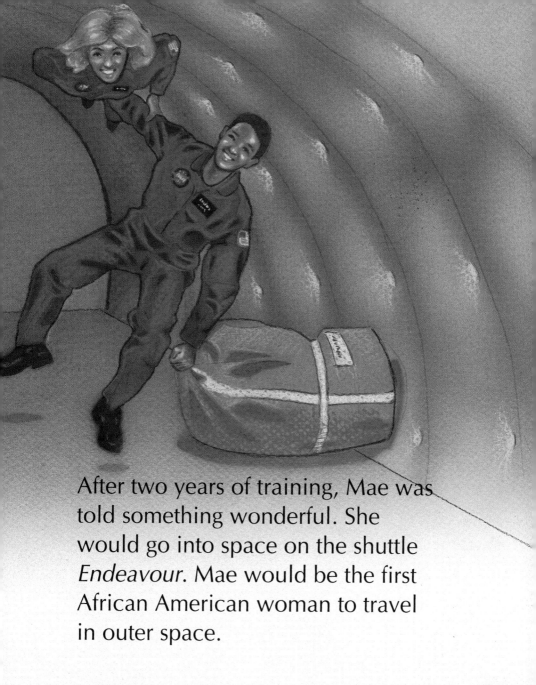

After two years of training, Mae was
told something wonderful. She
would go into space on the shuttle
Endeavour. Mae would be the first
African American woman to travel
in outer space.

Training for a shuttle flight means working very hard. Each person on a shuttle must learn how to do difficult jobs.

On the *Endeavour*, Mae would try to solve health problems people had in space. One problem was how to keep astronauts from feeling sick to their stomachs. Another problem was how to keep their bones strong. To prepare, Mae learned all she could about these problems.

On September 12, 1992, Dr. Mae Jemison dressed in her space suit and walked onto the shuttle *Endeavour.* Then she left the planet Earth for one week. She took along some of her treasures from Earth—pieces of art from Africa.

On the shuttle, Mae was among a crew of seven astronauts. There were five men and one other woman. One of the men was a Japanese astronaut. The United States and Japan were working together in outer space.

21

Dr. Mae Jemison no longer works for NASA. She left the space agency to teach people about science and health care. She also wants to convince countries of all sizes, all over Earth, that space exploration is for all peoples.

Mae Dreamed Of Being In Space

A five-year-old in awe,
Mae dreamed of being in space,
Of traveling past the stars,
And seeing comets race.

And then when Mae grew up,
She made her dream a fact.
Of all women astronauts,
Mae was the first one who was Black.

On a shuttle called *Endeavour*
She was shot out into space.
Dr. Mae Jemison
In history made a place.

Today Mae wants to work
Telling countries big and small
That race and sex don't count,
And outer space is for all.

Glossary

ancestor (an´ ses tər) The people in your family who lived long before you

astronaut (as´ trə nôt) A person trained to make rocket flights in outer space

Gemini (jem´ ə nī *or* jem´ ə¯ne) A set of space flights, in 1965 and 1966, carrying two men each time. The name means "twins."

NASA (nas´ ə) The National Aeronautics and Space Administration, which runs the U.S. space program

Peace Corps (pēs kôr) An organization from the United States that helps people in other countries

scientist (sī´ ən tist) A person who learns about and makes tests in science—the study of nature and the universe

shuttle (shut´ l) A space craft that carries astronauts into space and back to Earth, and can then be used again

About the Author

Garnet Jackson was born and raised in New Orleans, Louisiana. She is now an elementary school teacher in Flint, Michigan, with a deep concern for developing a positive self-image in young African American students. After an unsuccessful search for materials on famous African Americans written for early readers, Ms. Jackson produced a series of biographies herself. She has now written a second series. Besides being a teacher, Ms. Jackson is a poet and a newspaper columnist. She dedicates this book with love to her son Damon.

About the Illustrator

Fred Willingham has been a freelance artist since his graduation from the Art Institute of Pittsburgh in 1987. He has illustrated greeting cards and educational booklets, and he now has a limited edition of a fine art print on the market. He has used his favorite medium of air brush and pastels in *Mae Jemison*, with an eye for technical accuracy.